Ian Hamilton was born in 1938, in King's Lynn, Norfolk, and educated at Darlington Grammar School and Keble College, Oxford. In 1962, he founded the influential poetry magazine, the *Review*, and he was later editor of the *New Review*. Since then he has written biographies and ~~erature and football.~~

IAN HAMILTON

Sixty Poems

faber and faber

First published in 1998
by Faber and Faber Limited
3 Queen Square London WC1N 3AU

Photoset by Wilmaset Ltd, Wirral
Printed in England by Mackays of Chatham plc, Chatham, Kent

© Ian Hamilton, 1998

Ian Hamilton is hereby identified as author of this
work in accordance with Section 77 of the Copyright,
Designs and Patents Act 1988

A CIP record for this book
is available from the British Library

ISBN 0-571-19626-8

2 4 6 8 10 9 7 5 3 1

Contents

Sixty Poems

Memorial

Four weathered gravestones tilt against the wall
Of your Victorian asylum.
Out of bounds, you kneel in the long grass
Deciphering obliterated names:
Old lunatics who died here.

The Storm

Miles off, a storm breaks. It ripples to our room.
You look up into the light so it catches one side
Of your face, your tight mouth, your startled eye.
You turn to me and when I call you come
Over and kneel beside me, wanting me to take
Your head between my hands as if it were
A delicate bowl that the storm might break.
You want me to get between you and the brute thunder.
Settling on your flesh my great hands stir,
Pulse on you and then, wondering how to do it, grip.
The storm rolls through me as your mouth opens.

Pretending not to Sleep

The waiting rooms are full of 'characters'
Pretending not to sleep.
Your eyes are open
But you're far away
At home, *am Rhein*, with mother and the cats.
Your hair grazes my wrist.
My cold hand surprises you.

The porters yawn against the slot-machines
And watch contentedly; they know I've lost.
The last train
Is simmering outside, and overhead
Steam flowers in the station rafters.
Soft flecks of soot begin to settle
On your suddenly outstretched palms.
Your mouth is dry, excited, going home:

The velvet curtains,
Father dead, the road up to the village,
Your hands tightening in the thick fur
Of your mother's Persian, your dreams
Moving through Belgium now, full of your trip.

Trucks

At four, a line of trucks. Their light
Slops in and spreads across the ceiling,
Gleams, and goes. Aching, you turn back
From the wall and your hands reach out
Over me. They are caught
In the last beam and, pale,
They fly there now. You're taking off, you say,
And won't be back.
                              Your shadows soar.
My hands, they can merely touch down
On your shoulders and wait. Very soon
The trucks will be gone. Bitter, you will turn
Back again. We will join our cold hands together.

The Recruits

'Nothing moves,' you say, and stare across the lawn.
'The sun is everywhere. There will be no breeze.'
Birds line the gutters, and from our window
We see cats file across five gardens
To the shade and stand there, watching the sky.
You cry again: 'They know.'
The dead flies pile up on the window sill.
You shudder as the silence darkens, till
It's perfect night in you. And then you scream.

Windfalls

The windfalls ripen on the lawn,
The flies won't be disturbed.
They doze and glisten;
They wait for the fresh falls to wipe them out.

Birthday Poem

Tight in your hands,
Your Empire Exhibition shaving mug.
You keep it now
As a spittoon, its bloated doves,
Its 1938
Stained by the droppings of your blood.
Tonight,
Half-suffocated, cancerous,
Deceived,
You bite against its gilded china mouth
And wait for an attack.

Metaphor

Your shadows blossom now about your bed
Discolouring
The last irritated facts.
Your oriental dressing-gown;
Its golden butterflies, laced to their silken leaves,
Ache from the sudden darkness at your door.
You talk of butterflies, their luxuries, their skills
And their imprisonment.
You say,
'By these analogies we live.'

The sound of water trembles at the lip
Of this glass you are about to smash;
Your curtains flame like corrugated shields
Across these late September fields of snow
That are killing you.

Father, Dying

Your fingers, wisps of blanket hair
Caught in their nails, extend to touch
The bedside roses flaking in the heat.
White petals fall.

                  Trapped on your hand
They darken, cling in sweat, then curl,
Dry out and drop away.

                  Hour after hour
They trickle from the branch. At last
It's clean and, when you touch it, cold.
You lean forward to watch the thorns
Pluck on your skin white pools
That bleed as your fist tightens.
'My hand's in flower,' you say. 'My blood
Excites this petal dross. I'll live.'

Bequest

It is midwinter now and I am warm,
Bedridden, glad to be outlived.
My furniture
Surrounds me. I can reach my books.
And you, night after night
Until 'the end',
Will sit with me.

Between us
There are medicines, this pain
And these unfinished poems I bequeath you.
It must often be like this.
We darken gently as you count the days.
Your breath on mine,
Monotonously warm.

Midwinter

Entranced, you turn again and over there
It is white also. Rectangular white lawns
For miles, white walls between them. Snow.
You close your eyes. The terrible changes.

White movements in one corner of your room.
Between your hands, the flowers of your quilt
Are stormed. Dark shadows smudge
Their faded, impossible colours, but won't settle.

You can hear the ice take hold.
Along the street
The yellowed drifts, cleansed by a minute's fall,
Wait to be fouled again. Your final breath
Is in the air, pure white, and moving fast.

Last Respects

Your breathing slightly disarrays
A single row of petals
As you lean over him. Your fingers,
In the air, above his face,
Are elegant, perplexed. They pause
At his cold mouth
But won't touch down; thin shadows drift
On candle smoke into his hair.
Your friendly touch
Brings down more petals:
A colourful panic.

Funeral

The tall weeds trail their hair
And spiral lazily
Up from their barnacled black roots
As if to touch,
Though hardly caring,
The light that polishes their quiet pool.

Beyond this damp, unpopular beach
The funeral cars,
Bathed in their own light,
Are gliding home now
And the first spray is breaking on my skin.

This tolerant breeze will not disturb us,
Father and son. The hotel is alight.

Epitaph

The scent of old roses and tobacco
Takes me back.
It's almost twenty years
Since I last saw you
And our half-hearted love affair goes on.

You left me this:
A hand, half-open, motionless
On a green counterpane.
Enough to build
A few melancholy poems on.

If I had touched you then
One of us might have survived.

Complaint

I've done what I could. My boys run wild now.
They seek their chances while their mother rots here.
And up the road, the man,
My one man, who touched me everywhere,
Falls to bits under the ground.

I am dumpy, obtuse, old and out of it.
At night, I can feel my hands prowl over me,
Lightly probing at my breasts, my knees,
The folds of my belly,
Now and then pressing and sometimes,
In their hunger, tearing me.
I live alone.

My boys run, leaving their mother as they would a stone
That rolls on in the playground after the bell has gone.
I gather dust and I could almost love the grave.
To have small beasts room in me would be something.
But here, at eight again, I watch the blossoms break
Beyond this gravel yard.
I know how to behave.

Night Walk

Above us now, the bridge,
The dual carriageway,
And the new cars, their solemn music
Cool, expectant, happily pursued.
Tonight, your eyes half-closed, you want to lean
But patiently, upon my arm.

You want to sleep, imagining you see
Again thin-shadowed, anxious pools of light
Swarm quietly across this dark canal
And fade upon the weeds;
These soft horizons,
Softer than my touch.

Poem

Ah, listen now,
Each breath more temperate, more kind,
More close to death.
Sleep on
And listen to these words
Faintly, and with a tentative alarm,
Refuse to waken you.

Admission

The chapped lips of the uniformed night-porter
Mumble horribly against the misted glass
Of our black ambulance.
Our plight
Inspires a single, soldierly, contemptuous stare
And then he waves us on, to Blighty.

Last Waltz

From where we sit, we can just about identify
The faces of these people we don't know:
A shadowed semi-circle
Ranged around the huge, donated television set
That dominates the ward.

The 'Last Waltz' floods over them
Illuminating
Fond, exhausted smiles. And we,
As if we cared, are smiling too.

To each lost soul, at this late hour
A medicated pang of happiness.

Nature

I sit beneath this gleaming wall of rock
And let the breeze lap over me.
It's pleasant
Counting syllables in perfect scenery
Now that you've gone.

Home

This weather won't let up. Above our heads
The houses lean upon each other's backs
And suffer the dark sleet that lashes them
Downhill. One window is alight.

'That's where I live.' My father's sleepless eye
Is burning down on us. The ice
That catches in your hair melts on my tongue.

The Visit

They've let me walk with you
As far as this high wall. The placid smiles
Of our new friends, the old incurables,
Pursue us lovingly.
Their boyish, suntanned heads,
Their ancient arms
Outstretched, belong to you.

Although your head still burns
Your hands remember me.

The Vow

O world leave this alone
At least
This shocked and slightly aromatic fall of leaves
She gathers now and presses to her mouth
And swears on. Swears that love,
What's left of it,
Will sleep now, unappeased, impossible.

Your Cry

Your mouth, a thread of dying grass
Sealed to its lower lip,
At last is opening. We are alone,
You used to say,
And in each other's care.

Your cry
Has interrupted nothing and our hands,
Limp in each other's hair,
Have lost their touch.

Awakening

Your head, so sick, is leaning against mine,
So sensible. You can't remember
Why you're here, nor do you recognize
These helping hands.
My love,
The world encircles us. We're losing ground.

Aftermath

You eat out of my hand,
Exhausted animal. Your hair
Hangs from my wrist.

I promise that when your destruction comes
It will be mine
Who could have come between you.

Words

You've had no life at all
To speak of, silent child.
Tonight
Your mother's German lullaby
Broke into tears
Upon your dreamless head
And you awoke in joy
To welcome her unanswerable cry.

Old Photograph

You are wandering in the deep field
That backs on to the room I used to work in
And from time to time
You look up to see if I am watching you.
To this day
Your arms are full of the wild flowers
You were most in love with.

Neighbours

From the bay windows
Of the mouldering hotel across the road from us
Mysterious, one-night itinerants emerge
On to their balconies
To breathe the cool night air.

We let them stare
In at our quiet lives.
They let us wonder what's become of them.

Breaking Up

He's driving now,
The father of your family,
Somewhere up north. Before he left
You shared out your three hundred books
Together. He has taken those you've read
And left behind
Those you have secretly decided
Are unreadable.

Newscast

The Vietnam war drags on
In one corner of our living-room.
The conversation turns
To take it in.
Our smoking heads
Drift back to us
From the grey fires of South-east Asia.

Curfew

It's midnight
And our silent house is listening
To the last sounds of people going home.
We lie beside our curtained window
Wondering
What makes them do it.

Now and Then

The white walls of the Institution
Overlook a strip of thriving meadowland.
On clear days, we can walk there
And look back upon your 'second home'
From the green shelter
Of this wild, top-heavy tree.

It all seems so long ago. This afternoon
A gentle sun
Smiles on the tidy avenues, the lawns,
The miniature allotments,
On the barred windows of the brand-new
Chronic block, 'our pride and joy'.
At the main gate
Pale visitors are hurrying from cars.

It all seems so far away. This afternoon
The smoke from our abandoned cigarettes
Climbs in a single column to the sky.
A gentle sun
Smiles on the dark, afflicted heads
Of young men who have come to nothing.

Retreat

A minute pulsation of blood-red
Invades one corner of your wounded eye.
You hear it throb
In perfect harmony with our despair
And I'm no comfort to you any more.

Friends

'At one time we wanted nothing more
Than to wake up in each other's arms.'
Old enemy,
You want to live for ever
And I don't
Was the last pact we made
On our last afternoon together.

In Dreams

To live like this:
One hand in yours, the other
Murderously cold; one eye
Pretending to watch over you,
The other blind.

                We live in dreams:
These sentimental afternoons,
These silent vows,
How we would starve without them.

Bedtime Story

From your cautiously parked car
We watch the lights go out
Along this reputable cul-de-sac.

Your garden furniture
Sleeps in a haze of cultivated blossom
And the two trees you have been working on
All summer
Doze beside your garden gate.

'So many families. So many friends.'
In love at last, you can imagine them
Pyjama'd and half-pissed
Extinguishing another perfect day.

Poet

'Light fails; the world sucks on the winter dark
And everywhere
Huge cities are surrendering their ghosts...'
The poet, listening for other lives
Like his, begins again: 'And it is all
Folly...'

Critique

In Cornwall, from the shelter of your bungalow
You found the sea 'compassionate'
And then 'monotonous',
Though never, in all fairness,
'*Inconnue*'. There was no hiding it.
Your poems wouldn't do.

We sat on for another hour or two,
Old literary pals,
You chewing on your J & B
And me with your dud manuscripts
Face downward on my knee.

'It's been a long time,' you said,
'I'll race you to the sea.'

Ghosts

The scrubbed, magnificently decked coffin
Skates, like a new ship, into the fiery deep.
On dry land,
The congregation rustles to its knees.

From my corner pew
I command an unobstructed view
Of your departure.
If you had been lying on your side
I might have caught your unsuspecting eye.

Out on the patio, at dusk,
The floral tributes. I could almost swear
That it was you I saw
Sniffing the wreath-scented air
And counting the bowed heads of your bereaved.

Rose

In the delicately shrouded heart
Of this white rose, a patient eye,
The eye of love,
Knows who I am, and where I've been
Tonight, and what I wish I'd done.

I have been watching this white rose
For hours, imagining
Each tremor of each petal to be like a breath
That silences and soothes.
'Look at it,' I'd say to you
If you were here: 'it is a sign
Of what is brief, and lonely
And in love.'

But you have gone and so I'll call it wise:
A patient breath, an eye, a rose
That opens up too easily, and dies.

Anniversary

You have forgotten almost everything
We promised never to let go.
I even wonder if you know
Why at the dead of night you went with me
To face those blindly drifting gusts of snow,
Why it had to be that route we took
And not the other, why
After all that's gone between us
We still seem to be together.

In this deadeningly harsh weather
It's a waste of breath trying to explain
Over again. You walk ahead
Unsteadily. I let you. A red coat
Disappearing into snow; the green branch
You were carrying abandoned:
Separate lives
Now distantly marooned.
You're small, and smaller still
With every move you make.
In ten seconds we will hear it break.

Returning

It isn't far. Come with me. There's a path
We used to take. There is a stream,
A thin ripple, really, of white stones
Dislodged from a dilapidated boundary
Between two now-forgotten fields;
There is a tree, a muddily abandoned sprawl
Off-balance – the one tall thing
You could see from where I walked with her.

What it all looks like now I wouldn't know,
But come with me. It was an early dusk
On that day too, and just as sickeningly cold,
And when I called to her: 'It isn't far',
She said: 'You go.'
Somewhere ahead of us
I thought I could foresee
A silence, a new path,
A clean sweep of solitude, downhill.

Dear friend, I wish you could have seen
This place when it was at its best,
When I was,
But it isn't far. It isn't far. Come with me.

Remember This

You won't remember this, but I will:
A gradually tightening avenue of trees
And where it locks
What seems from here the most yearningly delicate
Intrusion of white leaves
May yet blacken the unclouded pool of sun
That summons you.
                              Keep going
Even though I mean to stay; keep going
Even though I can't any more imagine
What I'll find most hard to bear
On the way back from here,
On the way home
To where we first vowed we'd try again to say:
You won't remember this.

New Year

You are not with me, and for all I know
You may not have survived.
The weather's 'almost gone'
You used to say
And so it has.
                    Lost child
Look over there: this unprofitable
Three dozen yards of land, still fortified
Against non-residents, has had its day;
The trees you couldn't climb,
Fatigued, are clownishly spiked out
On an expressionless, half-darkened wall of sky.
Home far from home.

So far as I can see, none of it,
Nor of us, my love, minds much what's next to go:
Another lapse of the delighted heart
That's given up on you,
Another pleasantness to wait for, and then wait again,
Then wait; the infant lawns
You weren't supposed to walk on, semi-swamps
Of glitteringly drenched green.

Colours

Yes, I suppose you taught us something.
That bottle-green priest's dressing-gown,
For instance, that they tried to tog you up in
For your last overnight at the Infirmary.
'My Celtic shroud', you called it
And when no one laughed: 'Before morning
Your dear daddy will be Ibrox blue.'

Familiars

If you were to look up now you would see
The moon, the bridge, the ambulance,
The road back into town.
                              The river weeds
You crouch in seem a yard shorter,
A shade more featherishly purple
Than they were this time last year;
The caverns of 'your bridge'
Less brilliantly jet-black than I remember them.

Even from up here, though, I can tell
It's the same unfathomable prayer:
If you were to look up now would you see
Your moon-man swimming through the moonlit air?

Larkinesque

Your solicitor and mine sit side by side
In front of us, in Courtroom Number Three.
It's cut and dried,
They've told us, a sure-fire decree:
No property disputes, no tug-of-love,
No bitching about maintenance. Well done.

All that remains
Is for the Judge to 'wrap it up', and that's how come
We sit here, also side by side
(Although to each of us we are 'the other side'),
And listen to Forbes-Robertson and Smythe,
Our champions, relax.
                                It turns out, natch,
They went to the same school,
That neither of them ever thought
The other had it in him to ... and yet,
Well, here they were, each peddling
Divorces for a crust. Too bloody true.
And did not each of them remember well
Old Spotty Moses and his 'magic snake',
Mott Harrison's appalling breath, Butch Akenside's
Flamboyant, rather pushy suicide?
Indeed. Where were *they* now? (Aside,
That is to say, from Akenside.) Ah well.

'And you, old man, did you, well, take the plunge?'
No bloody fear: Forbes-Robertson, it seems,
Keeps Labradors, and Smythe keeps his relationships
'Strictly Socratic'. When you'd seen
What they'd seen ... and so on.

Their rhythms were becoming Larkinesque
And so would mine if I were made to do
This kind of thing more often. As it is,
The morning sun, far from 'unhindered', animates
The hands I used to write about with 'lyric force'.
Your hands
Now clutching a slim volume of dead writs.

The Forties

'The self that has survived those trashy years',
Its 'austere virtue' magically intact. Well then,
He must have asked himself, is this
The 'this is it'; that encapsulable Life
I never thought to find
And didn't seek: beginning at the middle
So that in the end
The damage is outlived by the repair?

At forty-five
I'm father of the house now and at dusk
You'll see me take my 'evening stroll'
Down to the dozing lily pond:
From our rear deck, one hundred and eleven yards.
And there I'll pause, half-sober, without pain
And seem to listen; but no longer 'listen out'.
And at my back,
Eight windows, a veranda, the neat plot
For your (why not?) 'organic greens',
The trellis that needs fixing, that I'll fix.

House Work

How can I keep it steady?
Don't you see
The weakened plank, dead-centre?
And I can't believe that you can fail to hear
This slight but certain tremor underfoot
When you steal in, so lovingly invisible,
To polish my condemned, three-legged desk.

The Garden

This garden's leaning in on us, green-shadowed
Shadowed green, as if to say: be still, don't agitate
For what's been overgrown —
Some cobbled little serpent of a path,
Perhaps, an arbour, a dry pond
That you'd have plans for if this place belonged to you.
The vegetation's rank, I'll grant you that,
The weeds well out of order, shoulder-high
And too complacently deranged. The trees
Ought not to scrape your face, your hands, your hair
Nor so haphazardly swarm upwards to impede
The sunlit air you say you need to breathe
In summertime. It shouldn't be so dark
So early.
             All the same, if I were you,
I'd let it be. Lay down your scythe. Don't fidget
For old clearances, or new. For one more day
Let's listen to our shadows and be glad
That this much light has managed to get through.

Again

That dream again: you stop me at the door
And take my arm, but grievingly.
Behind you, in the parlour, I can see
The bow of a deep sofa, blanketed in grey,
And next to it, as if at harbourside,
A darker grey, rough-sculpted group of three.
Three profiles sombrely inclined,
Long overcoats unbuttoned, hats in hand:
Night-mariners, with eyes of stone,
And yet the eyes seem stricken.
Is it that they too can hardly bear
What's happened? What *has* happened? Who?

At Evening

Arriving early, I catch sight of you
Across the lawn. You're hovering:
A silver teaspoon in one hand
(The garden table almost set)
And in the other, a blue vase.
For the few seconds I stand watching you
It seems half-certain you'll choose wrong
– Well, not exactly wrong, but dottily,
Off-key. You know,
That dreaminess in you we used to smile about
(My pet, my little lavender, my sprite),
It's getting worse.
I'd talk to you about it if I could.

Soliloquy

'We die together though we live apart'
You say, not looking up at me,
Not looking up.
                  'I mean to say,
Even were we actually to die in unison,
Evaporating in each other's arms,
We'd still have ended up – well, wouldn't we? –
Dying for a taste, our first and last,
Of unaloneness:
                  we'd have dreamed,
Dreamed up a day utterly unclouded
By the dread that not quite yet but soon,
Although, please God, not very soon,
We will indeed be whispering
Wretchedly, in unison, your breath on mine:
I might as well be dead,
Or we might. Do you follow? Are you
With me? Do you see?'

Steps

Where do we find ourselves? What is this tale
With no beginning and no end?
We know not the extremes. Perhaps
There are none.
We are on a kind of stair. The world below
Will never be regained; was never there
Perhaps. And yet it seems
We've climbed to where we are
With diligence, as if told long ago
How high the highest rung.
Alas: this lethargy at noon,
This interfered-with air.

Fever

We are dreaming of a shape within a blur:
A hairline thread, a fracture that won't knit,
A flaw that won't be fatal but won't fade.
We are dreaming of old damage, scars
That hold but never heal.
We are dreaming of discolorations,
Tubes the size of pinholes, mucky lungs.

We are dreaming of a dream within a dream:
A seaside sickroom breeze,
The blue curtains that lilt with it,
Floral walls. And in the air,
Anxiety, not ours.
I think we are dreaming of young mothers,
Of iodine, thermometers, cool hands.

Resolve

You used to know. You used to know
My other room, my books,
My altered times of day.
You used to know my friends.

You used to know how hard I tried
And how foolhardily I'd swear
That this time I'd not falter. You could tell
What lay in store for me, and what I'd spent
And what might be retrieved.

Enchantress, know-all, Queen of Numbers, Muse,
You knew all this. And what do you know now?
More of the same, you'll say,
But toothless, blind, forgetful. Well, perhaps.

Unlock my hand,
Let's call this 'for the last time'.
When you go,
Don't murmur, as you used to, 'Yes, I know.'

Dream Song

He called you Master of beauty,
Craftsman of the snowflake, your contrivances
Beyond compare, or competition.
He knew little of your character,
Your background, or your 'motivation'
Famously mysterious and manifold.

Most nights it was enough
To seek to praise, imploringly,
Your work so far, your imminent
Deep-thirsting rose,
For instance, your now dead
And yet triumphant to remember

Daffodil, your giant tree almost afloat
Again outside his window,
Punctual and unthrifty in its green.
Great Lord,
Was it indeed your will
That he should thus so humanly
Heartsore pick up his pen and look the other way?

Responsibilities

Imagining you on your own,
I'm vigilant.
You've heard me, I can tell.
A rustle in the kitchen leaves
Above your head, a semi-stifled click
Somewhere below, an errant chime
An hour or so into your sleeplessness:
Ghost tremors,
They don't keep you company,
Not now, and they won't bring me back,
Not this time. 'Please
Leave me alone,' I've heard you cry
And you have heard me rustle in reply,
Or click, or chime: 'Don't make me go.'

Biography

Who turned the page? When I went out
Last night, his Life was left wide-open,
Half-way through, in lamplight on my desk:
The Middle Years.
Now look at him. Who turned the page?